Facts About the Hamster

By Lisa Strattin

© 2019 Lisa Strattin

FREE BOOK

FREE FOR ALL SUBSCRIBERS

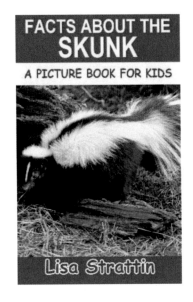

LisaStrattin.com/Subscribe-Here

BOX SET

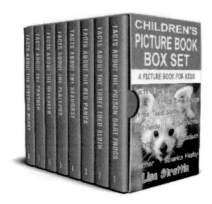

- **FACTS ABOUT THE POISON DART FROGS**
- **FACTS ABOUT THE THREE TOED SLOTH**
- **FACTS ABOUT THE RED PANDA**
- **FACTS ABOUT THE SEAHORSE**
- **FACTS ABOUT THE PLATYPUS**
- **FACTS ABOUT THE REINDEER**
- **FACTS ABOUT THE PANTHER**
- **FACTS ABOUT THE SIBERIAN HUSKY**

LisaStrattin.com/BookBundle

Facts for Kids Picture Books by Lisa Strattin

Little Blue Penguin, Vol 92

Chipmunk, Vol 5

Frilled Lizard, Vol 39

Blue and Gold Macaw, Vol 13

Poison Dart Frogs, Vol 50

Blue Tarantula, Vol 115

African Elephants, Vol 8

Amur Leopard, Vol 89

Sabre Tooth Tiger, Vol 167

Baboon, Vol 174

Sign Up for New Release Emails Here

LisaStrattin.com/subscribe-here

Contents

INTRODUCTION

Hamsters are thought to be originally from the desert lands of east Asia. In the wild, hamsters tend to spend most of their time digging burrows and foraging for food.

CHARACTERISTICS

Hamsters are solitary animals. Some types of hamsters want to be alone so much that they will fight to the death if more than one hamster is in the same territory!

Many species of hamster are very fast at running and are able to escape from predators. Because of the shape and size of their hind feet, they are often able to run as quickly backwards as they can forwards, which the allows them to escape easily in their burrows.

APPEARANCE

Hamsters, in a way, look like small bears. This is especially true when they stand up on their rear legs and start dancing around!

A hamster has bold and shiny eyes with large and upright ears. They usually have a round body, seeming to be quite plump.

LIFE STAGES

The gestation period can be between 16 to 30 days, depending on the species of hamster. Syrian hamsters can have up to 20 babies at one time, while most other hamsters have 10 or fewer. Hamsters can reach sexual maturity as early as one to two months old, but this is too young and often means that there can be health problems, both for the mother and babies.

LIFE SPAN

Hamsters live to be 2 to 3 years old, on average.

SIZE

There are more than 20 different species of hamster found in the wild (and even more in the commercial pet market).

The Russian dwarf hamster is among the smallest species of hamster with adult Russian dwarf hamsters rarely growing to more than 4 inches long.

The more common Syrian hamster is the largest species and some Syrian hamster individuals have been known to grow to nearly 12 inches long, although the average size of a Syrian hamster is normally around 6 inches long.

HABITAT

Hamsters in the wild are nocturnal. They spend the daytime hours in burrows underground in order to avoid the predators within their natural environment. The hamster leaves the safety of its underground burrow in the nighttime to search for food.

Hamsters live in semi-desert regions around the world with the soft ground providing the proper dirt for the hamster to burrow into. The burrow often consists of many tunnels and chambers, including separate areas where the hamster eats and sleeps.

DIET

Hamsters use their large cheek pouches to store food so that they can take the food back and stash it in their underground burrow. Nuts, seeds, vegetables, grass, fruits and berries are all part of their natural diet.

ENEMIES

Their predators are birds of prey like owls, animals of the dog family like coyotes and foxes, some snakes, wild cats, and in some parts of the world, humans. Wild hamsters don't really have a friendly relationship with any animal in their native environment.

SUITABILITY AS PETS

Hamsters are well-known to be great pets. They are small and easy to care for, with pet stores having proper food and habitats for them. If you want a small pet, a hamster is likely a great choice!

COLOR ME

COLOR ME

COLOR ME

COLOR ME

COLOR ME

COLOR ME

COLOR ME

COLOR ME

Please leave me a review here:

LisaStrattin.com/Review-Vol-247

For more Kindle Downloads Visit Lisa Strattin Author Page on Amazon Author Central

amazon.com/author/lisastrattin

To see upcoming titles, visit my website at LisaStrattin.com– most books available on Kindle!

LisaStrattin.com

FREE BOOK

FOR ALL SUBSCRIBERS – SIGN UP NOW

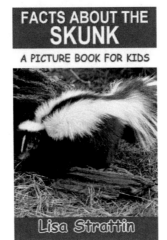

LisaStrattin.com/Subscribe-Here

LisaStrattin.com/Facebook

LisaStrattin.com/Youtube